MANAGEMENT OF AILMENTS THROUGH YOGA

Dr. Subramaniam Seshan Iyer

<u>Preface</u>

The book is designed to create awareness among common people the various methods through which different ailments can be treated. The focus is on Yoga practice to be adopted as Lifestyle in order to live 100 years. I would like to tell the readers that our body is designed to live more than 100 years but due to lifestyle we lose many years of our precious life.

I hope that this book will help all the people to get rid of their various ailments mentioned in the book.

<u>Acknowledgement</u>

I would like to acknowledge the support of my family members especially my wife who has always been an inspiration in all my endeavors.

I would also like to acknowledge Janardan Swami who has been my support in understanding various yoga practices and its usage.

I would also like to acknowledge Swami Ramdev whose program on television on yoga inspired me to present this book.

Last but not the least I would like to acknowledge my parents who at present are not with me but due to them I am living with a purpose.

<u>Index</u>

Chapter 1

Management of PCOD (Polycystic Ovary Disease)

Polycystic ovary disease (PCOD) could be a heterogeneous and for the most part unexplained disorder. The foremost widely accepted diagnostic criteria for PCOD are characterized by oligo/anovulation, physical or organic chemistry findings of hyperandrogenism and polycystic ovaries. Any 2 of the 3, while ruling out different potential unsupportive diagnoses, can award an identification of PCOD and all the potential implications that comes with this identification. A diagnosis of PCOD incurs a higher risk for infertility, cardiovascular disease, type 2 diabetes, and gynecological malignancies creating it imperative an applicable diagnosis is formed and subsequent screening modalities are followed.

Yoga has given new lease of life to many, so to treat various chronic diseases it is providing remedies which will be effective in your life. PATANJALI is providing a platform to practice Yoga. Yoga can give support to patients having polycystic ovary disease or syndrome through its numerous relevant postures (asana's) which can be done very simply. Yoga is a method with will relieve you from a particular disease. If it is performed each day it will add vital energy for smooth life even if the individual is suffering from any chronic disease. In this article 7 postures (asana's) will be provided which can be performed at any time in the day but early morning will always be preferred (empty stomach) to get good result. Yoga must be done after due consultation with your physician.

Introduction

Polycystic ovary syndrome (PCOS) could be a hormonal disorder common among ladies of generative age. Women with PCOS may have infrequent or prolonged menstrual periods or excess male hormone (androgen) levels. The ovaries develop numerous small collections of fluid (follicles) and are not able to regularly release eggs.

Symptoms

Common symptoms of PCOD include:

- Irregular periods or no periods at all.
- difficulty getting pregnant (because of irregular ovulation or failure to ovulate)
- Excessive hair growth (hirsutism) – usually on the face, chest, back or buttocks.
- Weight gain.
- Thinning hair and hair loss from the head.
- Oily skin or acne.

Cause of PCOD

The cause of PCOD is still unknown. PCOD is associated with low-grade inflammation, excess insulin, production of male hormones (Hyperandrogenism) in high quantity and genetics. Early age of menarche, indiscipline life system and pollution are some of the factors of PCOD.

Prevention

Foods to avoid

- Refined carbohydrates, such as mass-produced pastries and white bread.
- Fried foods, such as fast food.
- Sugary beverages, such as sodas and energy drinks.
- Processed meats, such as hot dogs, sausages, and luncheon meats.
- Solid fats, including margarine, shortening, and lard.

Asanas

Badhakonasana - Butterfly Pose

Step 1 - Sit on the floor on a yoga mat or a well carpeted area.
Step 2 – Keep your spine and legs straight.
Step 3 –Form a winged butterfly pose.
Step 4 – Feet should be brought towards the pelvis and you must join them subsequently holding with your hands.

Supta Badhakonasana (Reclining Bound Angle Pose)

Step 1

Perform Baddha Konasana. Exhale and lower the back torso toward the floor, first leaning on the hands. The moment leaning back on the forearms is done, use the hands to spread the back of the pelvis and release the lower back and upper buttocks through the tailbone. The torso must be brought all the way to the floor, supporting the head and neck on a blanket roll or bolster if required.

Step 2

Grip the topmost thighs with the hands and rotate the inner thighs externally, pressing the outer thighs away from the sides of the torso. Slide the hands along the outer thighs from the hips toward the knees and widen the outer knees away from the hips. Then slide the hands down along the inner thighs, from the knees to the groins. Realize that the inner groins are sinking into the pelvis. Push the hip points together, so that the back pelvis widens and the front pelvis narrows. Keep the arms on the floor, angled at about 45 degrees from the sides of the torso and keep the palms up.

Step 3

Realist that the knees are floating up toward the ceiling and continue settling the groins deep into the pelvis. As the groins drop toward the floor, so will the knees.

Step 4

Firstly, stay in this pose for one minute. Gradually extend the stay for five to 10 minutes. To come out of this posture use the hands to press the thighs together, then roll over onto one side and push away from the floor, head trailing the torso.

1. **Bharadwajasana**

a. Begin in Dandasana (Staff Pose); move the sacrum in and up toward the navel, and extend the sternum away from the navel to lengthen the front body.
b. Feel the pubis and tailbone dropping equally toward the

floor—the bowl of the pelvis is upright, neither spilling forward nor spilling back; also notice that the two sides of the waist are equally long.

c. Imagine a central axis running through the torso from the pelvic floor to the crown of the head.

d. Emphasize both the length and the integrity of this axis; the column is straight and is not tilting or curving off to one side or another.

e. Keeping the imprint of this central axis, lean onto the right hip and swing the legs to the left, bending the knees and placing the feet to the outside of the left hip.

f. Nestle the left ankle on top of the right arch, and descend the left sitting bone to recreate the evenness in the side body from Dandasana.

g. Inhale, and lengthen along the central axis.

h. Exhale, and twist the torso around that length to the right; keep the left sitting bone heavy.

i. Place the left hand beneath the right knee with the fingers pointed back toward the knee, and take the right hand to the floor behind the right hip.

j. Draw back with the head of the left upper arm so that the hand position doesn't cause the shoulder to hunch forward.

k. Take the gaze to the right, but make sure the twist in the neck is not happening at the expense of rotation throughout the spine and torso.

l. Continue the essential pattern of breath; use inhalations to lengthen and exhalations to twist any amount more.

m. Hold for 8–10 breaths, then release back to center.

n. Repeat on the other side.

Chakki Chalanasana – Churning Mill Pose[2]

a. To come in this asana, first sit in Dandasana (Staff pose). Sit keeping the legs straight in front of the body.

b. Now separate the legs as wide as possible. Without bending the knees and with the back straight.

c. After that join the palms with lock them together. And stretch out the arm at shoulder height in front of you. Make sure the elbows should not be bending.

d. Bend forward as far as possible and assume that you are

churning the mill with a home stone grinder.

e. Now, taking in deep breaths, move the hands in circular motion over the legs or you can do so in a clockwise direction.

f. You have to inhale while bending forward from the right and exhale as you go backward from the left.

g. In this position only the arms and the body moving clockwise and anticlockwise. You should be keeping the hips firm.

h. Keep breathing deeply and easily while rotating. You will feel the stretch in the arms, abs, groin and legs.

i. Do not overexert theself while practicing this Pose.

j. Repeat this asana anticlockwise direction.

k. After the practice, rest the body in Shavasana for 1-2 minutes.

Shavasana

a. Lie on the back with the legs straight and arms at the sides. Rest the hands about six inches away from the body with the palms up. Let the feet drop open. Close the eyes. You may want to cover the body with a blanket.

b. Let the breath occur naturally.

c. Allow the body to feel heavy on the ground.

d. Working from the soles of the feet up to the crown of the head, consciously release every body part, organ, and cell.

e. Relax the face. Let the eyes drop deep into their sockets. Invite peace and silence into the mind, body, and soul.

f. Stay in Savasana for five minutes for every 30 minutes of the practice.

g. To exit the pose, first begin to deepen the breath. Bringing gentle movement and awareness back to the body, wiggling the fingers and toes. Roll to the right side and rest there for a moment. With an inhalation, gently press theself into a comfortable seated position. Let the head be the last thing to come into place. Carry the peace and stillness of Savasana with you throughout the rest of the day.

Padmasadhana

To start first 10 minutes, do the following asana:

    a. For body rotation, sit in a half-lotus posture and rotate the body clockwise and anticlockwise, four times in each direction.

b. Lie down on the floor on the stomach to transition to Makarasana known as the crocodile pose where the head is raised, and the feet are perpendicular to the ground. This asana is for relaxation.

c. Gradually transition to the Ardha salabhasana by lifting the feet off the floor, one by one.

d. Move on to the Purna salabhasana by placing the palms under the pelvis and lifting both the limbs off the floor.

e. It is time now for the Bhujangasana where you keep both the hands near the shoulders and slowly bend back backwards. The Navel should remain on the floor, and the head should look up.

f. Transition to the Viprit Salabhasana keeping the stomach on the ground and lifting both the hands and legs off the floor.

g. Now hold both the feet with the hands making a bow shape with the body to perform the Dhanurasana.

The asanas must be followed by 5 minutes of anulom vilom and 20 minutes of meditation. Finally, complete it with 5 minutes of pranayama.

Sun Salutation / Surya Namaskar

Step 1 (Prayer Pose) – First stand on the edge of the mat and keep the feet together and balance the weight equally on both the feet. Expand the chest and relax the shoulders. As you breathe in, lift both arms up from the sides and as you exhale, bring the palms together in front of the chest in prayer position.

Step 2 (Raised Arms pose) – Keeping biceps close to the ears breath in and lift the arms up and back. Remain in the pose, objective is to stretch the whole body up from the heels to the tips of the fingers. To get maximum benefits, you may pull the pelvis forward and ensure reaching up with the fingers rather than going backwards.

Step 3 (Hand to Foot pose) - Breathing out, bend forward from the waist, keep the spine erect. As air is exhaled, bring the hands down to the floor, near the feet.

Step 4 (Equestrian Pose) - Breathing in, push the right leg back, as far back as possible. Bring the right knee to the floor and try to see upwards.

Step 5 (Stick pose) - First breathe in, take the left leg back and bring the whole body in a straight line and keep the arms perpendicular to the floor.

Step 6 (Saluting with eight points or parts) - Gently bring the knees down to the floor and exhale. Take hips backward slightly, slide forward, rest the chest and chin on the floor. Raise the posterior a little bit .The two hands, two feet, two knees, chest and chin (eight parts of the body) should touch the floor.

Step 7 (Cobra pose) - Slide ahead and raise the chest upwards into a cobra posture. You may keep the elbows bent in this pose, the shoulders away from the ears. Look up. Inhale air, make a gentle effort to push the chest forward; as air is exhaled, make a gentle effort to push the navel down. Tuck the toes under. Ensure the stretching is done as much as it can; avoid force.

Step 8 (Mountain pose) – Exhale air, lift the hips and the tail bone up, chest downwards in an 'inverted V' (/\) posture. If it is possible, try and keep the heels on the ground and make effort to lift the tailbone up, going deeper into the stretch.

Step 9 (Equestrian Pose) - Breathing in, push the right leg back, as far back as possible. Try to bring the right knee to the floor and look upwards.

Step 10 (Hand to foot pose) – Exhale and bring the left foot forward. Keep the palms on the floor. You may bend the knees, if necessary. Gently straighten the knees and if you can, try and touch the nose to the knees. Keep breathing.

Step 11 (Raised Arms pose) - Inhale, roll the spine up, hands go up and bend backwards a little bit, pushing the hips slightly outward. Ensure that the biceps are beside the ears. The idea is to stretch up rather than stretching backwards.

Step 12 - As you exhale, first straighten the body, and then bring the arms down. Relax in this position; observe the sensations in the body.

Benefits of Yoga in Polycystic Ovary Disease

1. Reduces Anxiety - Anxiety is common among women with PCOS and yoga may provide an effective and non-invasive treatment for women with the condition to manage it. It has been found that 12 weeks of a holistic yoga program in adolescent girls with PCOS was significantly better than a physical exercise program in reducing anxiety symptoms[3].

2. Improves Hormones - There is evidence to suggest that the benefits of yoga go beyond that of reducing anxiety for women with PCOS to improving sex hormones and regulating menstrual cycles. It has been found that adolescent girls with PCOS who are engaged in a holistic yoga program involving one hour of yoga daily for 12 weeks, showed significant improvement in anti-müllerian hormone, luteinizing hormone (LH), and testosterone, even more so than physical exercise. The girls who are practicing yoga daily

also are seeing improvements in <u>menstrual frequency</u>.

3. Improves metabolic markers - It seems that yoga can also have a positive impact on insulin and <u>cholesterol</u> levels in women with PCOS. Yoga was found to be effective than conventional physical exercises in improving glucose, lipid, and insulin resistance values among the girls with PCOS who practiced different varieties of yoga daily.

Conclusion

The research on Polycystic Ovary disease or Polycystic Ovary syndrome concludes that YOGA plays a vital role in maintaining the health. It also gives an impetus to the body to keep moving. All diseases sends a negative signal and to counter it YOGA plays a major role. The study gave an opportunity to understand the reasons for PCOD/PCOS and subsequently how YOGA can provide benefits. Everybody should take out time from there regimen to focus on YOGA as it will give an added energy to the vital organs and keep you healthy and fit. Secondly the postures recommended by the researcher is very simple and can be done by any age group person. The various YOGA poses will help you in leading a happy and stress free life. Keep doing it and stay healthy.

<u>Chapter 2</u>

<u>Treating of Joint Pain -</u>

<u>ARTHRITIS</u>

Arthritis is the swelling and tenderness of one or more of your joints. The main symptoms of arthritis are joint pain and stiffness, which typically worsen with age. Although there's no cure for arthritis, treatments have improved greatly in recent years and, for many types of arthritis, particularly inflammatory arthritis, there's a clear benefit in starting treatment at an early stage.

Cartilage is a firm but flexible connective tissue in your joints. It protects the joints by absorbing the pressure and shock created when you move and put stress on them. A reduction in the normal amount of this cartilage tissue cause some forms of arthritis.

Yoga is giving new lease of life to many, so to tackle chronic diseases it is providing remedies which will be effective for your entire life. It is delivered to many people by PATANJALI. Yoga can give support to patients having arthritis through its numerous relevant postures (asana's) which can be done very simply. Yoga does not send a message that if you do it regularly you will be relieved from a particular ailment. If it is performed each day it will add vital energy for smooth life even if you are suffering from any long term ailment. In this article we will be providing 5 postures (asana's) which can be performed at any time in the day but early morning will always be preferred (empty stomach) to get good result. Secondly this postures must be implemented after due consultation with your physician. If your physician disapproves don't do these postures as it will be harmful for your body.

Introduction

Arthritis is an inflammation of the joints. It can affect one joint or multiple joints. There are more than 100 different types of arthritis, with different causes and treatment methods. Two of the most common types are osteoarthritis (OA) and rheumatoid arthritis (RA).

The symptoms of arthritis usually develop over time, but they may also appear suddenly. Arthritis is most commonly seen in adults over the age of 65, but it can also develop in children, teens, and younger adults. Arthritis is more common in women than men and in people who are overweight.

Symptoms - Joint pain, stiffness, and swelling are the most common symptoms of arthritis. Your range of motion may also decrease, and you may experience redness of the skin around the joint. Many people with arthritis notice their symptoms are worse in the morning.

In the case of RA, you may feel tired or experience a loss of appetite due to the inflammation the immune system's activity causes. You may also become anemic — meaning your red blood cell count decreases — or have a slight fever. Severe RA can cause joint deformity if left untreated.

Causes

Cartilage is a firm but flexible connective tissue in your joints. It protects the joints by absorbing the pressure and shock created when you move and put stress on them. A reduction in the normal amount of this cartilage tissue cause some forms of arthritis.

Normal wear and tear causes OA, one of the most common forms of arthritis. An infection or injury to the joints can exacerbate this natural breakdown of cartilage tissue. Your risk of developing OA may be higher if you have a family history of the disease.

Another common form of arthritis, RA, is an autoimmune disorder. It occurs when your body's immune system attacks the tissues of the body. These attacks affect the synovium, a soft tissue in your joints that produces a fluid that nourishes the cartilage and lubricates the joints.

RA is a disease of the synovium that will invade and destroy a joint. It can eventually lead to the destruction of both bone and cartilage inside the joint.

[1]Diagnosis

Seeing your primary care physician is a good first step if you're unsure who to see for an arthritis diagnosis. They will perform a physical exam to check for fluid around the joints, warm or red joints, and limited range of motion in the joints. Your doctor can refer you to a specialist if needed.

If you're experiencing severe symptoms, you may choose to schedule an appointment with a rheumatologist first. This may lead to a faster diagnosis and treatment.

Extracting and analyzing inflammation levels in your blood and joint fluids can help your doctor determine what kind of arthritis you have. Blood tests that check for specific types of antibodies like anti-CCP (anti-cyclic citrullinated peptide), RF (rheumatoid factor), and ANA (antinuclear antibody) are also common diagnostic tests.

Doctors commonly use imaging scans such as X-ray, MRI, and CT scans to produce an image of your bones and cartilage. This is so they can rule out other causes of your symptoms, such as bone spurs.

Asanas

Balasana - Child Pose

1. Sit on your heels on a yoga mat or on the floor.
2. Either keep your knees together or apart.
3. Slowly, bend forward by lowering your forehead to touch the floor, exhaling as you **do** so.
4. Keep your arms alongside your body.

Bitilasana – Cow Pose

a. Start on your hands and knees in a "tabletop" position.
b. As you inhale, lift your sitting bones and chest toward the ceiling, allowing your belly to sink toward the floor.
c. Exhale, coming back to neutral "tabletop" position on your hands and knees.

Supta Matsyendrasana

a. Lie down on your back.

b. Bend your knees and put the soles of your feet on the floor with your knees pointing up toward the ceiling.

c. Press into your feet to lift your hips slightly off the floor and shift them about an inch to your right. This is an important step because it sets your hips up to stack one on top of the other when you move into the twist.

d. Exhale and draw your right knee into your chest and extend your left leg flat on the floor. Keep your left foot actively flexed throughout the pose. Inhale.

e. Exhale and cross your right knee over your midline to the floor on the left side of your body. Your right hip is now stacked on top of your left hip. You can hook your right foot behind your left knee if you like.

f. Open your right arm to the right, keeping it in line with your shoulders. Rest your left hand on your right knee or extend it to make a T shape with the arms. Turn your palms toward the ceiling.

g. Turn your head to the right, bringing your gaze over your shoulder to your right fingertips. You can skip this step if it doesn't feel good on your neck.

h. On your exhalations, release your left knee and your right shoulder toward the floor.

i. Hold the pose for five to 10 breaths. To come out of the pose, inhale and roll onto your back, drawing your right knee into your chest. Release both legs to the floor to neutralize your spine for several breaths before doing the other side.

Sethu Bandha Sarvangasana – Bridge Pose[2]

a. Lie on your back with your knees bent and the soles of your feet flat on the floor.

b. Extend your arms on the floor with your fingers reaching toward your heels. You should be able to just barely touch the backs of your heels with your fingertips.

c. Keep your feet parallel. Maintain that position throughout the pose.

d. Press down into the soles of your feet to lift your hips off the floor.

e. Slide your yoga block under your back directly under your sacrum, letting it rest securely on the bolster. Your arms can stay outstretched on the floor next to your body.

f. This should be a comfortable position. You may want to stay here several minutes as your body settles into the stretch and gets the benefits of a passive backbend. If the pose causes your back to hurt, remove the block and come down.

g. To come out, press down into your feet and lift your hips again. Slide the block out from under your sacrum and gently lower your back to the floor.

Anjaneyasana – Crescent Lunge

1. Begin in Tadasana (Mountain Pose) with your feet together and arms alongside your body. Distribute the weight evenly in your feet. If you have a hard time staying balanced here stand with the feet parallel and hip distance apart.

2. On an exhale step your left leg about 4 to 5 feet in back of you and come onto the back toes with the toes pointed straight forward. Try to get the heel hovering directly on top of those back toes.

3. You don't want to have your feet on a tightrope. For more stability you can walk the right foot out to the right a few inches. Keep the hips turned towards the front of your mat like two headlights pointing forward.

4. On an exhale, bend the right knee to 90 degrees so that the knee is directly over the ankle

and the shin is perpendicular to the earth. That knee should be in line with the second and third toe. Distribute the weight evenly through that front foot as you lift the inner arch and root down through the corners of the feet.

5. Engage the quad of the back leg. The back leg should be straight without locking out the knee.

   Modification: You may micro bend the back leg to create a bit more stability in the pose. You may also find the helps to square your hips towards the front of the room.

6. On an inhale, lift the arms up above head. Broaden the collarbones. Rotate the triceps or pinkie side of the hands in towards one another as you draw the shoulders away from the ears. Your fingers are actively reaching up towards the sky. Arms are either

      parallel to one another or palms are pressing together.

7. Lengthen the tailbone down towards the earth as you draw the navel gently in and up towards the spine. Tuck the lower ribs in.

8. Gaze forward and slightly upward. Make sure not to crunch the neck. You are rooting down to earth as you lengthen up towards the sky.

9. To get out of the posture, straighten the front leg, lower the arms and come back to mountain pose. Repeat on the left side.

Benefits of Yoga in Arthritis

a. Add variety to your workout – Yoga provides an exercise option. It may not be the only thing you do, but it can be a component of an overall healthy regimen that may also include cardiovascular exercises like walking or biking.

b. Improve physical function – People with arthritis who practice regularly will eventually see improved physical function.

c. Improve flexibility – Yoga can also benefit people with stiff joints due to arthritis. Stretching exercises in general help improve range of motion, so the fact that you're stretching in yoga will help flexibility.

d. Stay active- On days when you're experiencing a painful arthritis flare, continuing to do some type of physical activity like yoga, if possible, can help you maintain joint flexibility.

e. Create a mind body connection – Yoga's emphasis on introspective thought – pinpointing the sources of pain or anxiety and learning to relax them – is useful for people with arthritis. In yoga, you develop a communication with your own body.

Conclusion

The research on arthritis concludes that YOGA plays a vital role in maintaining your health. It also gives an impetus to your body to keep moving. Any ailment basically sends a negative signal and to counter it YOGA plays a major role. The study gave an opportunity to understand the reasons for Arthritis and subsequently how YOGA can provide benefits. Everybody should take out time from there regimen to focus on YOGA as it will give an added energy to your vital organs and keep you healthy and fit. Secondly the postures recommended by the researcher is very simple and can be done by any age group person. The various YOGA poses will help you in leading a happy and stress free life. Keep doing it and stay healthy.

Chapter 3

Management of Coronary Artery Disease through Yoga

Cardiovascular diseases are the leading cause of morbidity & mortality accounting for approximately 30% global burden of death per year. Disorders & in turn diseases due to gradual shifting towards sedentary lifestyle diseases like type 2 diabetes mellitus, hypertension, stroke, obesity etc are the major menacing factors for the progression of coronary artery disease. With speedy development of commerce and increased inclination towards lifestyle influenced by western countries in the past many years, prevalence of such diseases has reached frightening proportions among Indian population. Apart from physical consequences of cardiovascular diseases which are prominently looked for and taken care of, mental aspects of such patients are always overlooked. Such patients mentally become vulnerable & always remain worried & keep on feeling in their subconscious mind that soon they may die due to their heart condition. This in turn results into stress and anxiety which has become common amongst all the Indians. Medicines are commonest curative remedy in India but through this article, I am proposing some remedies through Yoga. This article doesn't guarantee 100% result, but it is preventive remedy for Coronary Artery Disease.

Introduction

When the major blood vessels (aorta, right coronary, left coronary, left anterior descending & circumflex) that supply heart get pathologically damaged, coronary artery disease develops. The most common cause for such pathological assault on coronaries is development of atheromatous plaques over their inner walls. Gradually it will lead to narrowing which in turn lead to partial or total block of the vessels. These blocks will limit or obstruct the blood supply to heart which will ultimately lead to ischemia to the heart. There are varieties of clusters of symptoms that will give indication of coronary heart disease. They are pain or discomfort (arms, left shoulder, back, neck, jaw or upper abdomen), breathlessness, palpitations, sweating, extreme weakness or anxiety. Various risk factors for coronary heart disease are:

- **Age:** as it advances, coronaries get narrowed and hardened.

- **Sex:** Comparatively women are protected but their risk increases after menopause.

- **Family history:** person is more susceptible if any close relative got any history of coronary heart disease.

- **Smoking:** smokers are at higher risk for developing coronary heart disease.

- **High blood pressure:** Uncontrolled blood pressure always result in hardening and narrowing of coronaries arteries.

- **High blood cholesterol levels:** there are higher chances of development of plaques which result in furtherance of atherosclerosis.

- **Diabetes:** Type 2 diabetics are more prone.

- **Obesity:** Excess weight typically worsens other risk factors.

- **Physical inactivity & High stress: They will worsen the situation.**

- **Unhealthy diet:** High amounts of saturated fat, trans fat, salt and sugar can increase your risk of coronary artery disease.

Prevention: The same lifestyle habits that can help treat coronary artery disease can also help prevent it from developing in the first place. Leading a healthy lifestyle can help keep your arteries strong and clear of plaque. To improve your heart health, you can: Quit smoking, stay physically active, Eat a low-fat, low-salt diet that's rich in fruits, vegetables and whole grains, Maintain a healthy weight, Reduce and manage stress. Yoga is giving a new lease of life to many, so to tackle chronic diseases it is providing remedies which will be lifelong. Yoga will provide support to patients having coronary artery disease through its various relevant postures (asana's) which can be done very easily. Yoga does not send a message that if you do it regularly you will be relieved from a particular disease. If it is performed every day it will add vital energy for smooth life even if you are suffering from any chronic disease. In this article we will be providing 6 postures (asana's) which can be performed at any time in the day, but early morning will always be preferred (empty stomach) to get good result. Secondly these postures must be implemented after due consultation with your physician. If your physician disapproves don't do these postures as it will be harmful for your body.

Asanas:

Utkatasana: It is also called as Chair Pose. Chair Pose clearly works the muscles of the arms and legs, but it also stimulates the diaphragm and heart. The steps are being given and it should be done maximum 10 times or as per your strength.

Step 1 - Stand in Tadasana. Inhale and raise your arms perpendicular to the floor. Either keep the arms parallel, palms facing inward, or join the palms.

Step 2- Exhale and bend your knees, trying to take the thighs as nearly parallel to the floor as possible. The knees will project out over the feet, and the torso will lean slightly forward over the thighs until the front torso forms approximately a right angle with the tops of the thighs. Keep the inner thighs parallel to each other and press the heads of the thigh bones down toward the heels.

Step 3- Firm your shoulder blades against the back. Take your tailbone down toward the floor and in toward your pubis to keep the lower back long.

Step 4- Stay for 30 seconds to a minute. To come out of this pose straighten your knees with an inhalation, lifting strongly through the arms. Exhale and release your arms to your sides into Tadasana.

Bhujangasana: Bhujangasana or Cobra Pose is a reclining back-bending asana in hatha yoga and modern yoga as exercise.

Step 1- Lie flat on your stomach on the floor. Stretch your legs back, tops of the feet on the floor. Spread your hands on the floor under your shoulders. Hug the elbows back into your body.

Step 2- Press the tops of the feet and thighs and the pubis firmly into the floor.

Step 3- On an inhalation, begin to straighten the arms to lift the chest off the floor, going only to the height at which you can maintain a connection through your pubis to your legs. Press the tailbone toward the pubis and lift the pubis toward the navel. Narrow the hip points. Firm but don't harden the buttocks.

Step 4- Firm the shoulder blades against the back, puffing the side ribs forward. Lift through the top of the sternum but avoid pushing the front ribs forward, which only hardens the lower back. Distribute the backbend evenly throughout the entire spine.

Step 5- Hold the pose anywhere from 15 to 30 seconds, breathing easily. Release back to the floor with an exhalation.

Makarasana:

Step 1: Lie down on the floor on your stomach. Fold your hands and keep the tip of the elbows on the ground with your fingers facing upwards. Keep your elbows shoulder distance apart.

Step 2: Now, raise your shoulders and head. Keep your neck straight and look ahead. Bend your head a little forward and place your chin in your palms.

Step 3: Stretch out your legs with the toes facing outwards. Feel your body touching the ground. Breathe normally and slowly and relax your muscles.

Step 4: Stay in the asana for a few minutes until you feel completely relaxed. To release from the position, gently remove your palms from the chin, bring your shoulders and head down, and roll over.

4. Padmasana:

Step 1: Sit on the floor with your legs straight in front. Bend your right knee and bring the lower leg up into a cradle: The outer edge of the foot is notched into the crook of the left elbow, the knee is wedged into the crook of the right elbow, and the hands are clasped (if possible) outside the shin. Lift the front torso toward the inner right leg so the spine lengthens (and the lower back does not round). Rock your leg back and forth a few times, exploring the full range of movement of the hip joint.

Step 2: Bend the left knee and turn the leg out. Rock your right leg far out to the right, then lock the knee tight by pressing the back of the thigh to the calf. Next swing the leg across in front of your torso, swiveling from the hip and not the knee, and nestle the outside edge of the foot into the inner left groin. Be sure to bring the right knee as close to the left as possible and press the right heel into the left lower belly. Ideally the sole of the foot is perpendicular to the floor, not parallel.

Step 3: Now lean back slightly, pick the right leg up off the floor, and lift the left leg in front of the right. To do this hold the underside of the left shin in your hands. Carefully slide the left leg over the right, snuggling the edge of the left foot deep into the right groin. Again, swivel into position from the hip joint, pressing the heel against the lower belly, and arrange the sole perpendicular to the floor. Draw the knees as close together as possible. Use the edges of the feet to press the groins toward the floor and lift through the top of the sternum. If you wish, you can place the hands palms up in jnana mudra, with the thumbs and first fingers touching.

Step 4: Padmasana is the sitting asana par excellence, but it's not for everybody. Experienced students can use it as a seat for their daily pranayama or meditation, but beginners may need to use other suitable positions. In the beginning, only hold the pose for a few seconds and quickly release. Remember that Padmasana is a "two-sided pose," so be sure to work with each leg crosses each time you practice. Gradually add a few seconds each week to your pose until you can sit comfortably for a minute or so. Ideally you should work with a teacher to monitor your progress.

5. Shavasana:

Step 1. Lie on your back with your legs straight and arms at your sides. Rest your hands about six inches away from your body with your palms up. Let your feet drop open. Close your eyes. You may want to cover your body with a blanket.

Step 2: Let your breath occur naturally. Allow your body to feel heavy on the ground.

Step 3: Working from the soles of your feet up to the crown of your head, consciously release everybody part, organ, and cell.

Step 4: Relax your face. Let your eyes drop deep into their sockets. Invite peace and silence into your mind, body, and soul. Stay in Shavasana for five minutes for every 30 minutes of your practice.

Step 5: To exit the pose, first begin to deepen your breath. Bringing gentle movement and awareness back to your body, wiggling your fingers and toes. Roll to your right side and rest there for a moment. With an inhalation, gently press yourself into a comfortable seated position. Let your head be the last thing to come into place. Carry the peace and stillness of Shavasana with you throughout the rest of your day.

6. Pawanmuktasana:

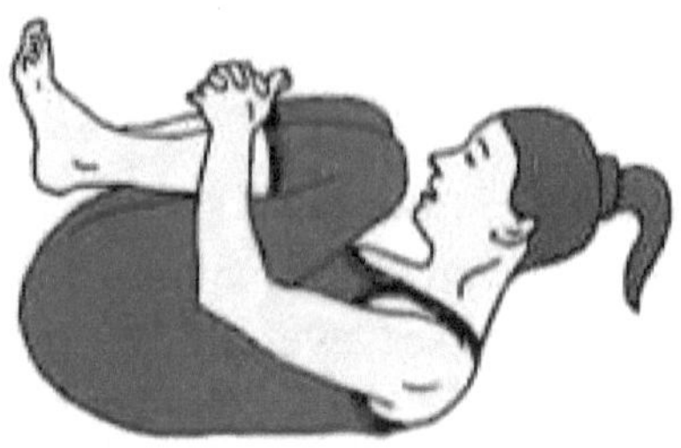

Step 1: Lie flat on your back on a smooth surface, ensuring that your feet are together, and your arms are placed beside your body.

Step2: Take a deep breath. As you exhale, bring your knees towards your chest, and press your thighs on your abdomen. Clasp your hands around your legs as if you are hugging your knees.

Step 3: Hold the asana while you breathe normally. Every time you exhale, make sure you tighten the grip of the hands on the upper shins, and increase the pressure on your chest. Every time you inhale, ensure that you loosen the grip.

Step 4: Exhale and release the pose after you rock and roll from side to side about three to five times. Relax.

Benefits of Yoga in coronary heart disease:

1. It tones your digestive organs and heart.
2. Stretches chests and lungs, open the heart and lungs.
3. It relaxes your body completely and keeps you rejuvenated.
4. It calms the brain, increase awareness and attentiveness.
5. It helps to lower blood pressure, calms the brain and helps relieve stress and mild depression, lastly relaxes the body.
6. Strengthens the abdominal muscle, massages the intestine and internal organs of digestive system, and improves digestion.

Conclusion:

Current research on coronary artery disease and its implication concludes that Yoga plays a vital role in maintaining your health. It also gives an impetus to your body to keep moving. Any disease basically sends a negative signal and to counter it, Yoga plays a major role. The study gave an opportunity to understand the reasons for coronary artery disease and subsequently how Yoga can provide benefits to a common man. Everybody should take out time from there regimen to focus on Yoga as it will give an added energy to your vital organs and keep you healthy and fit. Secondly the postures recommended by the researcher is very simple and can be done by any age group person. The various Yoga poses will help you in leading a happy and stress-free life. Keep doing it and stay healthy and keep your heart strong.

Chapter 4

Maintaining control over blood

sugar

Diabetes is a common disease in India and is making a huge impact on the health of an individual. People suffering from diabetes often are scared and afraid that they are not going to survive. On the positive side diabetes makes you disciplined and makes your routine quite systematic. The intake of foods is systematic and time to time, secondly regular exercise is also followed resulting into people getting into healthy mode. The major diabetes in India is either generic or stress. Life has become so stressful that people of age 35 – 45 are having blood sugar problem on a regular basis. Secondly life is so hectic that people are unable to take time out from their regular to do exercise resulting health hazards.

In this research paper, I will be addressing certain Yoga postures which will help people suffering from diabetes to have a systematic and health life. In addition these yoga postures will keep him fit and also energetic.

As you know diabetes is an ailment where there is lot of restrictions with respect to food intake which reduces the overall energy of the individual. These yoga postures will allow them to regain this energy.

Introduction

In my family my grandfather and father had diabetes so it has been a regular practice on my part to get my blood test on a regular basis. The reason is many people say diabetes is generic. I live in lot of stress thinking that in future I may have the same problem. I have seen my father living a much disciplined life after blood sugar was detected. He used to take medicine regularly and also do his walking or exercise very systematically. Expecting the same from me at this moment is very difficult as life is very hectic and taking time out to doing exercise is not easy.

Findings – The participants in the conduct of research were of the age group 25 – 45 years.

In the research program around 30 – 35 regular participants participated. The participants were suffering from Non-insulin dependent Diabetes Mellitus and were taking medicines regularly (one tablet twice a day of METFORMIN – 500 mg). The fasting and post meal of all the participants were collected before the implementation of yoga asana and after 10 weeks of completion of course of Yoga. The blood sugar reading of the 20 regular participants who did their asana systematically as recommended by the researcher and were present on all days in the 10 week program were as given under –

Normal values –

Fasting – 60 – 110 mg/dL

Postprandial – upto 160 mg/dL

Participant	Before yoga		After yoga	
	Fasting	Postprandial	Fasting	Postprandial

1	126.50	217.6	100.68	189.6
2	168.6	415.52	146.8	289.68
3	117.8	200	98.69	164.50
4	127	164	107	120
5	136	270	99	177
6	144	179.60	121	163
7	136	189.36	124	178.6
8	132.63	168.56	114	143
9	128.73	182.55	113	164
10	147	313	128.69	264.86
11	153	225	139.22	196.33
12	133	242	122	182
13	122	146	102	114
14	132	162	111	139
15	112	158	94	145
16	173	302	144	178
17	113	186	78	126
18	126	181	93	159
19	116	152	98	138
20	133	166	118	154

The researcher conducted two sample paired t-test to analyze the data collected before yoga and after yoga. The details of the t-test is presented –

BEFORE YOGA

T-Test result:

S. No		
1	t-score	6.1286
2	Standard Error of Difference	12.588
3	Degree of Freedom	19
4	Two tailed p-value	0

Confidence range:

1. Mean Difference - -77.1465
2. Confidence range – (- 103.4932) – (- 50.7998)

AFTER YOGA

T-Test result:

S. No		
1	t-score	7.3657
2	Standard Error of Difference	7.6944
3	Degree of Freedom	19
4	Two tailed p-value	0

Confidence range:

1. Mean Difference - -56.6745
2. Confidence range – (- 72.7789) – (-40.5701)

The yoga asana done by the participant for 10 weeks are described in detail. If a diabetic patient conducts sincerely these asana he will definitely control his sugar.

Asanas

Dhanurasana (Bow Pose)

This asana can be done by lying down in your stomach. Keep your hands on the side and then lift both the legs upward. Now hold the ankle with your hands and lift yourself upwards. Keep a smile on your face and keep yourself in the same position for 15 seconds. In the meantime inhale and exhale, come in normal lying position and relax.

Balasana or Child Pose is a reclining back-bending asana in hatha yoga and modern yoga as exercise.

Sit on your knees and try to touch your heel to the hips. Now stretch your hands and bend down as much as you can. Remain in this position for 15 seconds. Keep inhaling and exhaling during the entire asana.

Bhujangasana (Upward facing Dog Pose)

Lie down on the floor on your stomach. Keep your hands with palm down on the side of your neck and then lift yourself upwards. The pressure should be given to the legs in order to lift. Face should be upwards and keep inhaling and exhaling slowly. Remain in this position for 15 seconds. You can repeat it 10 – 20 times depending upon your energy.

Shavasana (Corpse Pose)

Lie down straight on your back and keep your eyes closed. This asana must be done for atleast 30 minutes. You must remain calm slowly inhaling and exhaling during the asana. It is a type of meditation in a lying position. You must relax stress slowly during this asana.

Viparita Karani (legs up the wall)

Lie down beside the wall and keep a soft pillow under your neck. Raise your legs alongside the wall keeping ad 90 degree. Remaining in this position for 5 to 10 minutes. Your neck, chin and throat must be relaxed during this asana.

Tadasana (Mountain Pose)

Stand straight on the flat ground and keep your arms on the sides of your body. Keep your palm in the upward direction. Slowly breathe in and extend your arms up and down to the sides of your body. Hold this position for a while. Repeat this position ten times. Exhale slowly and bring down your arms back in the starting position.

Mandukasana (Frog Pose)

Fold your knees backward and sit down on the ground with the assist of your knees. Make a fist and put your hand on your stomach. Keep your fist in such a way that the joint of your fists comes at the navel. Place your fist firmly and press your stomach. Bend forward in this position and try to touch the ground with your forehead. Hold this position for 15-20 seconds then, exhale and relax.

Chakrasana (Wheel Pose)

Lie down on your back. Bend your knees and bring your legs close to your hips. Bring your palm under your shoulder such that your fingers point towards your shoulders. Keep your elbows in shoulder-width apart. Press your palm firmly on the ground and inhale while lifting your shoulders, elbows, and hips. Straighten your arms and legs so that your hips and shoulder feel the upward push. Hold this pose for few seconds then, bend your elbows and shoulders first to bring your head down. After that, bend your knees to lower your hips and spine to the ground.

- Practice yoga under qualified professional
- Vigorous exercise and fast-paced yoga are done in hot temperature conditions. These are not recommending for patients with diabetes and heart diseases.
- Beginners to yoga should avoid hard yoga practices.
- Diabetic patients should regularly monitor their body reactions after every physical activity.
- Any sign or symptom or pain should not be overlooked if you are diabetic.

- Don't do yoga beyond your capabilities.
- Generally, yoga requires an empty stomach, but diabetic patients should take light snacks to avoid <u>hypoglycemia</u>.
- Any sign of dizziness, headache, etc. should be reported to the practitioner.

Benefits of Yoga in Diabetes

1. It tones your digestive organs and heart.
2. Stretches chests and lungs, open the heart and lungs.
3. It relaxes your body completely and keeps you rejuvenated.
4. It calms the brain, increase awareness and attentiveness.
5. It helps to lower blood pressure, calms the brain and helps relieve stress and mild depression, lastly relaxes the body.
6. Strengthens the abdominal muscle, massages the intestine and internal

organs of digestive system, and improves digestion.

Conclusion

The research on diabetes disease and its implication concludes that YOGA plays a vital role in maintaining your health. It also gives an impetus to your body to keep moving. Any disease basically sends a negative signal and to counter it YOGA plays a major role. The study gave an opportunity to understand the reasons for diabetes and subsequently how YOGA can provide benefits to a common man. Everybody should take out time from there regimen to focus on YOGA as it will give an added energy to your vital organs and keep you healthy and fit. Secondly the postures recommended by the researcher is very simple and can be done by any age group person. The various YOGA poses will help you in leading a happy and stress free life. Keep doing it and stay healthy and keep your blood sugar under control.
LIVE A HEALTHY LIFE.

Chapter 5
Management of Thyroid issues

Thyroid is a problem in India which is affecting around 4.2 crore people and the main cause of this is iodine deficiency. Thyroid majorly happens in women aged between 36 and 45 years. Thyroid is a lifelong disease which is required to be maintained but there is no complete cure. Thyroid is diagnosed in patients having TSH level above 5.0 uIU/ml. The major concern in women suffering from thyroid problem is physical consequences like obesity and expanded belly area. The confidence level in patients comes down and many people remain in the house refusing to go out. The numbers is increasing every year and it is high time to tackle the problem. Medicines are available for prevention but in this article I am proposing certain yoga postures that may be a remedy. The article does not guarantee 100% result but it is preventive remedy to patients suffering from thyroid.

Introduction

Hyperthyroidism is indeed a condition where the thyroid gland produces an excessive amount of thyroid hormone. This can lead to various symptoms such as weight loss, rapid heartbeat, sweating, nervousness, and irritability, among others. It can be caused by conditions such as Graves' disease, thyroid nodules, or inflammation of the thyroid gland (thyroiditis). Treatment options may include medications, radioactive iodine therapy, or surgery, depending on the underlying cause and severity of the condition.

Thyroid disease is indeed quite common, and its prevalence is higher among certain demographic groups, particularly women.

The risk factors you mentioned, such as family history, certain medical conditions, medication use, age and past treatments, can indeed increase the likelihood of developing thyroid disorders.

Family history plays a significant role, as there can be a genetic predisposition to thyroid disorders. Additionally, certain autoimmune conditions, such as Type 1 diabetes, lupus and rheumatoid arthritis, are associated with an increased risk of thyroid disease due to their autoimmune nature. Medications containing high levels of iodine, like amiodarone, can affect thyroid function and increase the risk of thyroid disorders in susceptible individuals.

Age is also a factor, particularly in women, as hormonal changes associated with menopause can impact thyroid function. Moreover, past treatments for thyroid conditions or thyroid cancer, such as thyroidectomy or radiation therapy, can affect thyroid function and increase the risk of developing thyroid disorders later in life.

It is essential for individuals with risk factors or symptoms suggestive of thyroid disease to undergo appropriate screening and monitoring by healthcare professionals for early detection and management of thyroid disorders.

Excess levels of thyroid hormones, as seen in hyperthyroidism, can indeed lead to various symptoms due to the accelerated metabolism. Some of the common symptoms include –

1. Nervousness and anxiety: Excess thyroid hormones can affect the nervous system, leading to increased feelings of nervousness, anxiety, and irritability.

2. Hyperactivity: Hyperthyroidism can cause an individual to feel restless and unable to stay still, manifesting as hyperactivity and a constant sense of nervous energy.

3. Unexplained or unplanned weight loss: Accelerated metabolism can result in weight loss, even without

changes in diet or physical activity. This weight loss may occur despite increased appetite.

4. Goitre: The thyroid gland may enlarge due to over activity, leading to the formation of a visible lump or swelling in the neck known as a goiter. This enlargement can sometimes cause discomfort or difficulty swallowing.

These symptoms can vary in severity and may not always be present in every individual with hyperthyroidism. It's essential for individuals experiencing these symptoms to seek medical evaluation and appropriate treatment to manage the condition and prevent complications.

Prevention: The same lifestyle habits that can help treat thyroid disease can also help prevent it from developing in the first place. Leading a healthy lifestyle can help keep your thyroid in control. To improve your heart health, you can: Quit smoking, Stay physically active, Eat a low-fat, low-salt diet that's rich in fruits, vegetables and whole grains, Maintain a Healthy weight, Reduce and manage stress. Yoga is giving a new lease of life to many, so to tackle chronic diseases it is providing remedies which will be lifelong.

Yoga will provide support to patients having thyroid disease through its various relevant postures (asana's) which can be done very easily. Yoga does not send a message that if you do it regularly you will be relieved from a particular disease. If it is performed every day it will add vital energy for smooth life even if you are suffering from any chronic disease. In this article we will be providing 6 postures (asana's) which can be performed at any time in the day but early morning will always be preferred (empty stomach) to get good result. Secondly this postures must be implemented after due consultation with your physician. If your physician disapproves don't do these postures as it will be harmful for your body.

Literature Review

The thyroid gland is responsible for producing thyroid hormones, which play a vital role in maintaining overall health and well-being. However, thyroid problems can arise when the thyroid gland becomes overactive (hyperthyroidism) or underactive (hypothyroidism). Yoga has been recognized as a complementary therapy for thyroid disorders, offering potential benefits in managing and even curing these conditions. Research suggests that yoga can have a positive impact on thyroid health. (Catherine Woodyard, 2011)

By activating the parasympathetic nervous system and inducing a relaxation response, yoga can help lower cortisol levels and reduce stress on the thyroid gland. (Catherine Woodyard, 2011)

Yoga encourages one to relax, slow the breath and focus on the present, shifting the balance from the sympathetic nervous system and the flight-or-fight response to the parasympathetic system and the relaxation response. The latter is calming and restorative; it lowers breathing and heart rate, decreases blood pressure, lowers cortisol levels, and increases blood flow to the intestines and vital organs. One of the main goals of yoga is to achieve tranquility of the mind and create a sense of well-being, feelings of relaxation, improved self-confidence, improved efficiency, increased attentiveness, lowered irritability, and an optimistic outlook on life. (Catherine Woodyard, 2011)

All studies reported positive effects in favor of the yoga interventions. There were moderate treatment effects with respect to 5 pain (SMD = −0.74 [CI: −0.97 to −0.52], P < 0.0001), and pain-related disability (SMD = −0.79 [CI: −1.02 to −0.56], P < 0.0001). Despite some study limitations, there was evidence that yoga may be useful for several pain-associated disorders. Thus, well-designed larger scale studies with adequate controls for confounding factors and more thorough statistical analyses are needed to verify these promising findings. (Arndt

Büssing, Andreas Michalsen, Sat Bir S. Khalsa, Shirley Telles, Karen J. Sherman *Hindawi Publishing Corporation,* **2012**
A recent research is reviewed on the effects of yoga poses on psychological conditions including anxiety and depression, on pain syndromes, cardiovascular, autoimmune and immune conditions and on pregnancy. Further, the physiological effects of yoga including decreased heartrate and blood pressure and the physical effects including weight loss and increased muscle strength are reviewed. Finally, potential underlying mechanisms are proposed including the stimulation of pressure receptors leading to enhanced vagal activity and reduced cortisol. (Tiffany Field **2011)**

Along with medications & yogic exercises, the patient needs good emotional and psychological care by the family members. The results however depend on the age, determination to get healthy frequency of yogic exercises in a day and particular asanas/ styles. Carson et.al (2007) reported that breast cancer patients who were more engaged in yogic exercises each day used to experience better relief, no pain, distress and greater relaxation in a day as compared to patients who practice less. (Nidhi Verma *Redshine Publication,* **2017**)

Yoga encourages one to relax, slow the breath and focus on the present, shifting the balance from the sympathetic nervous system and the flight-or-fight response to the parasympathetic system and the relaxation response. The latter is calming and restorative; it lowers breathing and heart rate, decreases blood pressure, lowers cortisol levels, and increases blood flow to the intestines and vital organs. One of the main goals of yoga is to achieve tranquility of the mind and create a sense of well-being, feelings of relaxation, improved self-confidence, improved efficiency, increased attentiveness, lowered irritability, and an optimistic outlook on life. (Catherine Woodyard *Medknow,* **2011**)

In the hatha yoga ashtanga tradition (the eight limb Patanjali Yoga), three of the limbs are meditation, breath work (pranayama) and physical postures (asana), which are widely practiced in yoga classes.

The benefits of yoga for mental and physical health are rooted in the practice's origins: in yoga, stress is said to be the root of all diseases. The established fields of psychoneuroimmunology and immune psychiatry study the interplay between the immune system and mood or mental states. (Carolina Estevao *Elsevier BV,* **2022**)

Many chronic conditions, including heart disease, cancer, and rheumatoid arthritis, are associated with underlying chronic inflammatory processes. Literature reviews have analyzed a variety of integrative therapies and their relationships with chronic inflammation. This systematic review is unique in reporting solely on yoga's relationship with inflammation. Its purpose was to synthesize current literature examining the impact of yoga interventions on inflammatory biomarkers in adults with chronic inflammatory-related disorders. Searches of several electronic databases were conducted. (Dilorom M. Djalilova, Paula Schulz, Ann M. Berger, Adam J. Case, Kevin Kupzyk, Alyson Ross *SAGE Publishing,* **2018**)

The role of yoga in curing thyroid problems is still being researched, but there is evidence to suggest that certain yoga practices can have a positive impact on thyroid. (Büssing et al., 2012)

Hypothesis –

H_1 - It is hypothesized that regular yoga practice can have a positive impact on thyroid disease, particularly hypothyroidism.

H_2 – Yoga practice does not play any positive impact on thyroid disease.

Data collected –

The research comprised of data collection of 25 persons suffering from thyroid issue of various age group. 5 patients were between age group 40 – 50, 10 patients were between age group 30 – 40 and remaining 10 patients were above 50 years. All the patients were female. The patients underwent TSH, T_3 and T_4 test before yoga asana and after yoga asana. The data received is shown in the Table no. 1.

Normal TSH – 0.5 to 5.0 mIU/L

Normal T_3 Level – 80 – 220 ng/dl

Normal T_4 level – 5.0 to 12.0 µg/dl

Age group	Patient Number	Before yoga			After yoga			Difference		
		TSH (mIU/L)	T3 (ng/dl)	T4 (µg/dl)	TSH (mIU/L)	T3 (ng/dl)	T4 (µg/dl)	TSH (mIU/L)	T3 (ng/dl)	T4 (µg/dl)
30 – 40	1	2.5	100	5	2.0	90	5	-0.5	-10	0
	2	3.0	85	5	3.0	85	5	No	0	0
	3	6.2	85	5.2	4.5	85	5.2	-1.7	0	0
	4	5.8	87	5.4	5.0	87	5.0	-0.8	0	-0.4
	5	5.0	92	8	5.0	82	6.0	No	-10	-2.0
	6	1.0	98	7	1.0	98	7	No	0	0
	7	6.0	120	8	4.6	90	6.5	-1.4	-30	-1.5
	8	3.25	125	6	3.0	115	6	-0.25	-10	0
	9	5.5	100	6	3.0	100	6	-2.5	0	0
	10	3.8	95	5.3	3	95	5.3	-0.8	0	0
40 – 50	1	5.2	235	14	4.5	165	8	-0.7	-70	-6
	2	5.8	100	6	3	100	6	-2.8	0	0
	3	4.6	98	5.5	3	98	5.5	-1.6	0	0
	4	5.5	230	16	5.0	180	12	-0.5	-50	-4
	5	6.0	85	5.0	5.6	85	5.0	-0.4	0	0
Above 50 years	1	6.2	250	15	4.5	220	12	-1.7	-30	-3
	2	6.0	245	16	4.6	145	13	-1.4	-100	-3
	3	6.7	240	15	5.3	155	13	-1.4	-85	-2
	4	6.5	95	6.0	5.4	95	6.0	-1.1	0	0
	5	6.8	98	8.0	6.0	88	8.0	-0.8	-10	0
	6	7.2	85	8.0	5.5	85	8.0	-1.7	0	0
	7	7.5	98	8.5	5.5	80	8.5	-2.0	-18	0
	8	6.0	235	13	5.8	210	9	-0.2	-25	-4
	9	6.2	225	14	5.8	160	8	-0.4	-65	-6

10	6.0	100	6.0	4.5	100	6.0	-1.5	0	0

ASANAS

1. All the patients suffering from Thyroid disease must do **UJJAYI** Pranayama. Ujjayi pranayama is done –

   Keep your mouth closed, but your lips soft. Concentrate on the sound of your breath; allow it to soothe your mind. It should be audible to you, but not so loud that someone standing several feet away can hear it. Let your inhalations fill your lungs to their fullest expansion.

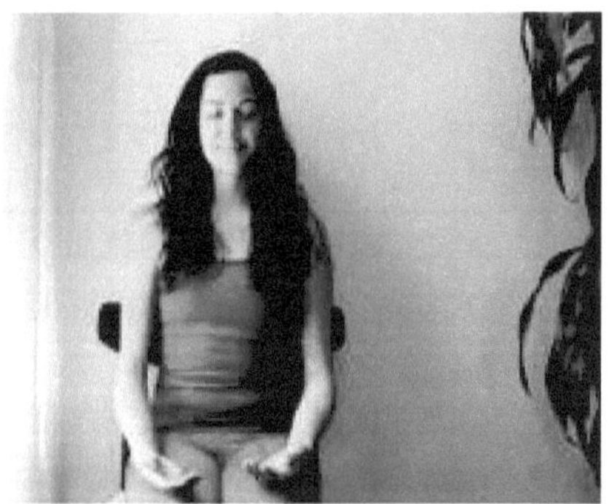

Figure - 1

Benefits of Ujjayi Pranayama

- lows the pace of the breath, which is said to improve longevity
- Cleanses and refreshes the nadis (subtle channels of the body)
- Infuses the mind-body with fresh prana (vital life force)
- Promotes mental clarity and focus
- Enhances memory
- Bolsters the immune system
- Improves skin color and complexion
- Soothes and rejuvenates the nervous system
- Promotes sound sleep
- Supports proper fluid balance in the tissues
- Fosters a profound sense of calm and relaxation in the mind and body
- Cleanses the emotional body by releasing stagnant emotions held in the tissues.

When to avoid Ujjayi Pranayama – if you are feeling tired, anxious or you are panicking. Beginners should not do this pranayama for more than 5 minutes

2. The next important asana is **SIMHASANA** Pranayama. Simhasana Pranayama is done –

Inhale through your nose. Exhale strongly through the mouth, making a "ha" sound. As you exhale, open your mouth wide and stick your tongue as far out as possible towards your chin. Try bringing your drishti (internal focus) towards your third eye (center of your forehead) or the tip of your nose as you exhale.

Figure - 2

Benefits of Simhasana –

1. It strengthens your back and reduces back pain.
2. It stretches your spine and improves the posture.
3. It reduces the issue of constipation as it improves the digestive system of the body.
4. The muscles of face and throat relaxes due to this asana.
5. People who perform this asana on a regular basis find their vocal cords opening and have a clear voice.

When to avoid doing Simhasana pranayama – if the person had a surgery of ankles, spine or knees, and if any person have a serious injury must avoid this asana.

3. **Bhujangasana** - Bhujangasana or Cobra Pose is a reclining back-bending asana in hatha yoga and modern yoga as exercise.

Figure 3

Step 1

Lie flat on your stomach on the floor.
Stretch your legs back, tops of the
feet on the floor. Spread your hands
on the floor under your shoulders.
Hug the elbows back into your body.

Step 2

Press the tops of the feet and thighs
and the pubis firmly into the floor.

Step 3

On an inhalation, begin to straighten
the arms to lift the chest off the floor,

going only to the height at which you can maintain a connection through your pubis to your legs. Press the tailbone toward the pubis and lift the pubis toward the navel. Narrow the hip points. Firm but don't harden the buttocks.

Step 4

Firm the shoulder blades against the back, puffing the side ribs forward. Lift through the top of the sternum but avoid pushing the front ribs forward, which only hardens the lower back. Distribute the backbend evenly throughout the entire spine.

Step 5

Hold the pose anywhere from 15 to 30 seconds, breathing easily. Release back to the floor with an exhalation.

When to avoid Bhujangasana – if you have undergone an abdominal surgery this asana must be avoided. Patients suffering from ulcers or hernia must not do this asana. Persons having spondylitis must avoid bhujangasana.

4. The next asana recommended in thyroid disease is **SARVANGASANA**. Sarvangasana is done –

    a. Lie down flat on your back. Keep your legs close together and your chin tucked in.
    b. Breathe deeply. Inhale. Lift your legs upwards till your feet are pointing.
    c. Tuck your hands underneath yourself with your palms facing up. With your hands under your buttocks, prepare to raise your torso.
    d. Lift your torso gradually till you are resting on your shoulders.
    e. Your arms must now be bent at the elbow. Bring your hands to your back to support yourself. Your legs should be over your head.
    f. Slowly straighten your back.
    g. Keep your knees firm but relax your calf muscles now. Maintain the posture.

h. To relax, lower your legs till your feet are at an angle of 45 degrees over your head. Lower your arms to the floor. Unwind gradually.

Figure 4

Benefits of Sarvangasana –

a. The circulation of blood in the body improves if you continuously do Sarvangasana.
b. It protects you from cardiovascular diseases.
c. It cures neurological and mental ailments.
d. It betters muscle strength.
e. The functions of thyroid gland is balanced if Sarvangasana is continuously done.

When to avoid Sarvangasana - If one has weak internal organs like the spleen, liver, kidney, or an enlarged thyroid should avoid this yoga pose. Patients having heart problem also must avoid Sarvangasana.

5. Another asana recommended in thyroid is **USTRASANA**. Ustrasana is done –

    a. Assume a kneeling position on a mat and support the body on the knees and toes (bent).
    b. Slowly, lean backwards, and take the arms behind.
    c. Fix the palms to the ground, with the fingers pointing outward and the thumb towards the toes.
    d. Keep the arms straight, eyes open, gaze fixed at a point.

Figure - 5

Benefits of Ustrasana –

    a. The entire body gets stretched resulting into relaxation.
    b. It helps in reducing extra fat in the body in patients suffering from Thyroid.
    c. It helps in the overall posture, as today we find many people suffer due to wrong posture.
    d. It makes your back muscles stronger.
    e. It helps to remove anxiety.

When to avoid Ustrasana – people suffering from high & low blood pressure, insomnia, back injury, pain in the neck or migraine must avoid Ustrasana.

6. Another asana that helps in thyroid disease is **MATSYASANA**.

Matsyasana is done –

    a. Begin by lying down on your back.
    b. Come up to your elbows with your forearms flat on the mat and your upper arms perpendicular to the floor.

c. Keep your forearms in place and puff up your chest by rolling your shoulders back and tucking your shoulder blades firmly onto your back.

Figure 6

Benefits of Matsyasana –

i. The fish pose encourages blood flow to thyroid gland and thus is good for people suffering from hyperthyroidism.

ii. It helps to manage asthma and bronchitis.

   iii.   It helps to control menstrual flow and manages menstrual pain in women.

   iv.   It helps to keep spine flexible and improves blood circulation.

   v.   If you do this asana regularly it relives from the problem of constipation by regularizing bowel movement.

When to avoid Matsyasana – people who suffer from low or high blood pressure, neck injury, injured lower back, or migraine must avoid Matsyasana.

Conclusion - Current research on thyroid disease and its implication concludes that Yoga plays a vital role in maintaining your health. It also gives an impetus to your body to keep moving. Any disease basically sends a negative signal and to counter it, Yoga plays a major role. The study gave an opportunity to understand the reasons for thyroid disease and subsequently how Yoga can provide benefits to a common man. Everybody should take out time from there regimen to focus on Yoga as it will give an added energy to your vital organs and keep you healthy and fit. Secondly the postures recommended by the researcher is very simple and can be done by any age group person. The various Yoga poses will help you in leading a happy and stress free life. Keep doing it and stay healthy and keep your heart strong.